I AM LEARNING THE ABLUTION AND DAILY PRAYERS

I AM LEARNING THE ABLUTION AND DAILY PRAYERS

Written by

Ümit Yıldırım

Published by Tughra Books
345 Clifton Ave., Clifton,
NJ, 07011, USA

www.tughrabooks.com

Project Editor: Betül Ertekin
Translated by Abdurrahman Çam
Illustrated by İsmail Abay
Graphic Design: İbrahim Akdağ

ISBN: 978-1-59784-283-9

Printed by
Çağlayan A.S. Izmir, Turkey

Dear Parents,

It is our duty to teach our children the beautiful aspects of our religion through our words and deeds. We should be patient in doing this. Repetition and teaching through demonstration will help them understand.

Our children will learn how to perform ablution and the Daily Prayers easily, with the help of this book.

It is highly recommended to study this work with your children, explaining the details. Of course, they will need some time to digest the information.

We hope that this book will play an important role in your children's spiritual development.

I'M LEARNING TO MAKE
ABLUTION (*WUDU*)

Murad and his family live in a beautiful small town. This town is full of colorful flowers and trees full of fruit.

But best of all is its amazing tiny mosque.

When night falls, the minaret's lights brighten up its surroundings. Out in its courtyard, the mosque has a pink fountain with three taps. Everyone makes *wudu* there before entering the mosque.

The imam of the mosque has a beard as white as snow. Everyone calls him Khalil Hodja. When the time comes, he calls the *adhan* from the minaret, his voice echoing throughout the town.

One day, Khalil Hodja invited the children of the town to the mosque.

Murad wore nice clean clothes and went to the mosque with great excitement. He wondered what Khalil Hodja was going to tell them.

When Murad entered the mosque's front gate, he heard the cheerful voices of his friends. They were jumping up and down with joy in the courtyard. A red-beaked bird was also there, flying around them.

Khalil Hodja greeted them at the mosque's front door: "Welcome, children! I have been waiting for you," he said smiling.

"Today, I'm going to teach you how to make *wudu*. Bushra, watch! Watch your friends closely, and later I will ask you to make *wudu*, too," said Khalil Hodja. Murad and Fuad went next to the fountain and folded their trousers up to their knees.

Khalil Hodja began explaining:

"First, let's wash our hands. Then, with our right hand, let's take water to our mouth three times. We will rinse our mouth with this water three times."

18

"Now it's time for our nose. Again, with our right hand, we will give water to our nose three times. Then, let's wash our face three times, this time using both hands."

Murad and Fuad carefully followed Khalil Hodja's instructions. He then continued:

"Now, it's time for our arms. First we wash our right arm then our left arm, including both elbows, three times each."

"To wet your hair, wet your right hand and wipe it over the top of your head," said Khalil Hodja. He was explaining and also carefully watching the two boys.

"Next, to clean our ears, wet both your hands. Wipe the inside of your ears with your pinkies and the outside with your thumbs. Also wet your nape with the back of your hands."

"Now it's time for our feet. We first wash our right foot, then the left one, both up to and including our ankles. Don't forget to wash in between your toes!"

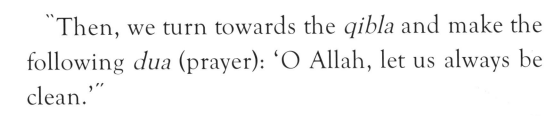

"Then, we turn towards the *qibla* and make the following *dua* (prayer): 'O Allah, let us always be clean.'"

The children repeated Khalil Hodja's prayer and said "Amin." Then, Bushra made *wudu*, too.

Khalil Hodja said in a serious manner, "Children, we have made our *wudu*, but to be able to pray, we can't break our *wudu*."

Bushra then asked, "How can *wudu* be broken?"

Khalil Hodja replied, "Listen very carefully," and continued explaining: "*Wudu* is broken if one uses the bathroom, bleeds or lets out any other dirty liquid, laughs during the Prayer, vomits, faints, passes gas or sleeps."

Then, rubbing his white beard, he said: "Now I'm going to recite a poem to you about *wudu*."

Making wudu with water and soap
Allah's pleasure our only hope
First in line we face the qibla,

Then we make our silent intention
Our hands and face will start the pace
Then mouth and nose is how it goes
Right arm, left arm, all over the forearm
Head, ears and nape, is before the final check
Then its right foot, left foot, three times repeat

Last of all, is a lesson rather small
And that's during wudu, we don't mix the order,
We don't talk, or waste any water.

The children liked the poem very much and clapped for Khalil Hodja.

Khalil Hodja smiled, "I'm glad you liked my poem. Now all of you have learned how to make *wudu*. Congratulations!"

"Later on, I will also teach you how to pray. Now, wait for me, I have a surprise for all of you," he added.

Then he went to the small shed by the mosque and returned with a small box in his hands.

"Close your eyes and hold out your hands," he said.

All of the kids were very excited. When they opened their eyes, they found colorful lollipops in their palms.

"Thank you Khalil Hodja!" they said.

Murad and his friends thanked Khalil Hodja. After finishing their lollipops, they played in the mosque's courtyard. To cool down afterwards, they washed their faces at the mosque's fountain.

That day, Murad and his friends were very happy to have learned how to make *wudu*.

I'M LEARNING TO PERFORM
THE DAILY PRAYERS (*SALAH*)

Murad saw a strange dream one night. In his dream, he was swimming in a river flowing pleasantly. Around him, fish were jumping in joy. During his dream, Murad felt very happy.

When he woke up in the morning, he explained his dream to his mom and dad with great excitement.

While explaining his dream, he remembered the words of the Prophet that he had just learned from Khalil Hodja at the mosque yesterday: "If a river flowed in front of your house and you washed yourself in it five times a day, would any dirt be left on you? See, the Daily Prayers are just like this."

"Murad, I guess what you learned at the mosque has really affected you," Murad's dad said.

"Yes, Dad! And today, we're also going to learn how to pray!" Murad said excitedly.

"Very good, Murad. Don't forget to thank Khalil Hodja, too," he said.

Murad replied "Okay" in a hurry and quickly got ready and left for the mosque.

The mosque's surroundings were decorated with flowers. It was as if all the flowers on the road were welcoming Murad inside.

And the butterflies! They were flying around Murad in joy. All this increased Murad's happiness. He couldn't wait to learn how to pray!

He immediately made *wudu* at the fountain outside the mosque and then went in. Khalil Hodja was reading the Qur'an.

At that moment, the beautiful decorations on the ceiling caught Murad's eye. They looked very lovely.

A short time later, his friends also made their way to the mosque.

Khalil Hodja called them next to him. "Children, today I am going to teach you how to pray," he said. "First, Murad and Bushra will stand on the Prayer rugs. Fuad should watch. You must do exactly as I say."

Murad and Bushra quickly stepped onto the Prayer rugs, ready to start.

Khalil Hodja started explaining, "Before starting the Prayer, you must turn towards the *qibla* and make your intention. Boys raise their hands up to their ears while girls raise their hands only up to their shoulders."

"After you make your intention, boys put their right hand over their left, below the belly button while girls keep theirs at chest level."

"Also, your eyes should be looking down at the point where your head will be at *sajdah* (prostration) when you put your forehead on the ground."

Murad and Bushra had already tried praying before by watching their parents. Because of this, they were able to follow Khalil Hodja's directions without making any mistakes.

Khalil Hodja continued, "Once we have held our hands together, we recite Subhanaka, Al-Fatiha and some verses from the Qur'an. Then we bend down and place our hands on our knees. This is called *ruku*. Girls don't need to bend down as much as the boys. Also, when in *ruku*, we praise Allah three times."

"When *ruku* finishes, we stand back up again. Then, we go to *sajdah*. This is where we place our forehead on the ground."

Khalil Hodja was just about to tell the children how their hands needed to be placed when Bushra said, "Our arms need to be like this, right?"

"Bushra, you shouldn't talk during the Prayer. If you talk, your Prayer will be cancelled," Khalil Hodja kindly answered.

"Sorry, I won't talk again."

"Ok, ok, but you just talked again," said Khalil Hodja smiling. Then he continued:

"When in *sajdah*, boys' arms will be tilted out slightly, while girls place their arms firmly on the ground. Then you say a certain phrase three times. Repeat this action and phrase one more time. Then stand back up. In this way, you have just completed one unit, or *rak'ah*, of the Prayer."

At this time, Fuad came to Khalil Hodja and asked him, "After two units we sit down, right?"

"Yes Fuad! Then we sit down and pray to Allah," Khalil Hodja said. Then he sat down on the floor.

"In this position, your hands are placed on top of your knees. Boys gently bend the toes on their right foot and girls tilt their feet slightly to the right. When we finish the Prayer while sitting, we say *salam* to our right first, and then to our left."

Murad raised his hand, "When making *salam* we say '*assalamu alaykum wa rahmatullah*,' right?"

"Yes, Murad! It seems you have been watching your elders, too, when they pray."

Around this time, Bushra finished her Prayer and asked, "Can I talk now?"

Khalil Hodja smiled, "Of course you can talk. Once you make *salam*, your Prayer finishes and you are free to talk."

Then it was Fuad's turn to pray. With his Prayer, everyone went over the things they had learned.

Khalil Hodja was watching them. A butterfly then landed on Murad's head. "Oh, what a beautiful butterfly!" Fuad said.

"I thought you couldn't talk during the Prayer! How quickly did you forget what you have learned!" Khalil Hodja said.

Then Murad asked a question: "Sometimes when my dad is praying, my little brother or sister climbs on his back. Is my dad's Prayer cancelled when my brother or sister does this?"

Khalil Hodja smiled at Murad and answered: "No, your dad's Prayer will be okay. But he might confuse the prayers he reads. Also your little brother or sister might slip and fall off, making your dad very sad."

Bushra joined in: "I try to pray every day by looking at my parents. Then I make a nice long *dua* afterwards. In the prayer I always say, 'O Allah! Bless my parents with health. Let them always be next to me.'"

Khalil Hodja said, "That is a very good prayer" and then all of them said "*Amin*" altogether. Before the children returned home, they thanked Khalil Hodja for another great day they spent together learning.